HAL LEONARD

GUITAR METHOD

Supplement to Any Guitar Method

EASY POP ME...

SECOND EDITION

INTRODUCTION

Welcome to *Easy Pop Melodies*, a collection of 20 pop and rock favourites arranged for easy guitar. If you're a beginning guitarist, you've come to the right place; these well-known songs will have you playing, reading, and enjoying music in no time!

This collection can be used on its own or as a supplement to the *Hal Leonard Guitar Method* or any other beginning guitar method. The songs are arranged in order of difficulty. Each melody is presented in an easy-to-read format—including lyrics to help you follow along and chords for optional accompaniment (by your teacher, if you have one).

USING THE CD

Easy Pop Melodies is available as a book/CD package so you can practice playing with a real band. On the CD, each song begins with a full (or partial) measure of clicks, which sets the tempo and prepares you for playing along. To tune your guitar to the CD, use the tuning notes on the final track (21).

Exclusive Distributors:
Music Sales Limited
8/9 Frith Street, London W1D 3JB, England.
Music Sales Pty Limited
120 Rothschild Avenue, Rosebery, NSW 2018, Australia.

Order No. HLE90002000
ISBN 1-84449-309-1
This book © Copyright 2004 by Hal Leonard Europe

Printed in the USA

Your Guarantee of Quality
As publishers, we strive to produce every book to the highest commercial standards.
This book has been carefully designed to minimise awkward page turns and to make playing from it a real pleasure.
Throughout, the printing and binding have been planned to ensure a sturdy, attractive publication which should give years of enjoyment.
If your copy fails to meet our high standards, please inform us and we will gladly replace it.

www.musicsales.com

HAL LEONARD EUROPE
DISTRIBUTED BY MUSIC SALES

SONG STRUCTURE

The songs in this book have different sections, which may or may not include the following:

Intro
This is usually a short instrumental section that "introduces" the song at the beginning.

Verse
This is one of the main sections of a song and conveys most of the storyline. A song usually has several verses, all with the same music but each with different lyrics.

Chorus
This is often the most memorable section of a song. Unlike the verse, the chorus usually has the same lyrics every time it repeats.

Bridge
This section is a break from the rest of the song, often having a very different chord progression and feel.

Solo
This is an instrumental section, often played over the verse or chorus structure.

Outro
Similar to an intro, this section brings the song to an end.

ENDINGS & REPEATS

Many of the songs have some new symbols that you must understand before playing. Each of these represents a different type of ending.

1st and 2nd Endings
These are indicated by brackets and numbers. The first time through a song section, play the first ending and then repeat. The second time through, skip the first ending, and play through the second ending.

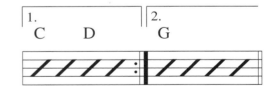

D.S.
This means "Dal Segno" or "from the sign." When you see this abbreviation above the staff, find the sign (𝄋) earlier in the song and resume playing from that point.

al Coda
This means "to the Coda," a concluding section in the song. If you see the words "D.S. al Coda," return to the sign (𝄋) earlier in the song and play until you see the words "To Coda," then skip to the Coda at the end of the song, indicated by the symbol: ⊕.

al Fine
This means "to the end." If you see the words "D.S. al Fine," return to the sign (𝄋) earlier in the song and play until you see the word "Fine."

D.C.
This means "Da Capo" or "from the head." When you see this abbreviation above the staff, return to the beginning (or "head") of the song and resume playing.

CONTENTS

Can You Feel The Love Tonight

from Walt Disney Pictures' THE LION KING

Words by TIM RICE
Music by ELTON JOHN

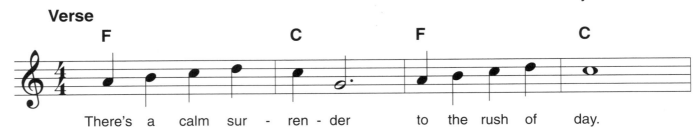

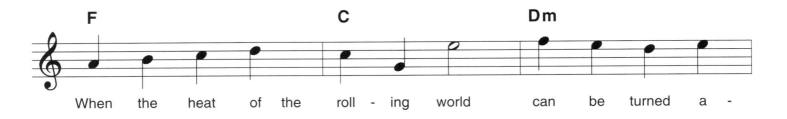

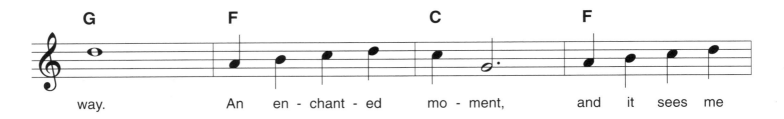

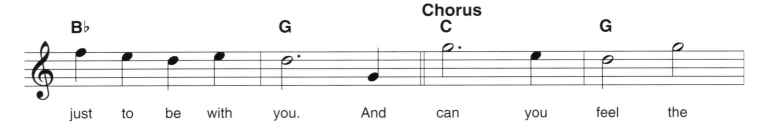

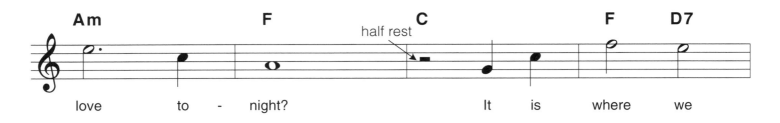

MULL OF KINTYRE

Words and Music by
MCCARTNEY-LAINE

LET IT BE

Words and Music by
JOHN LENNON and PAUL McCARTNEY

Verse

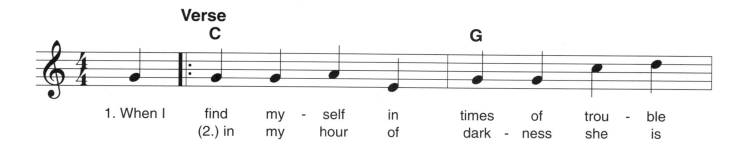

1. When I find my - self in times of trou - ble
(2.) in my hour of dark - ness she is

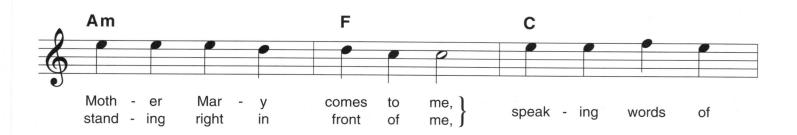

Moth - er Mar - y comes to me,
stand - ing right in front of me, } speak - ing words of

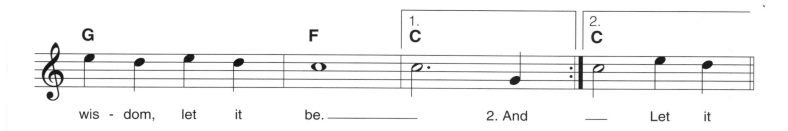

wis - dom, let it be. _____ 2. And _____ Let it

Chorus

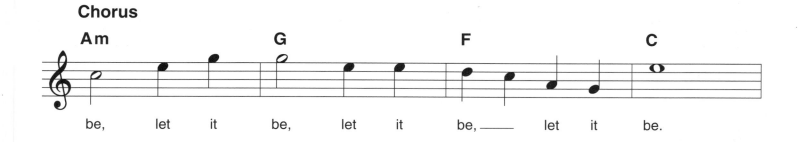

be, let it be, let it be, _____ let it be.

Whis - per words of wis - dom, let it be. _____

Your Cheatin' Heart

Words and Music by
HANK WILLIAMS

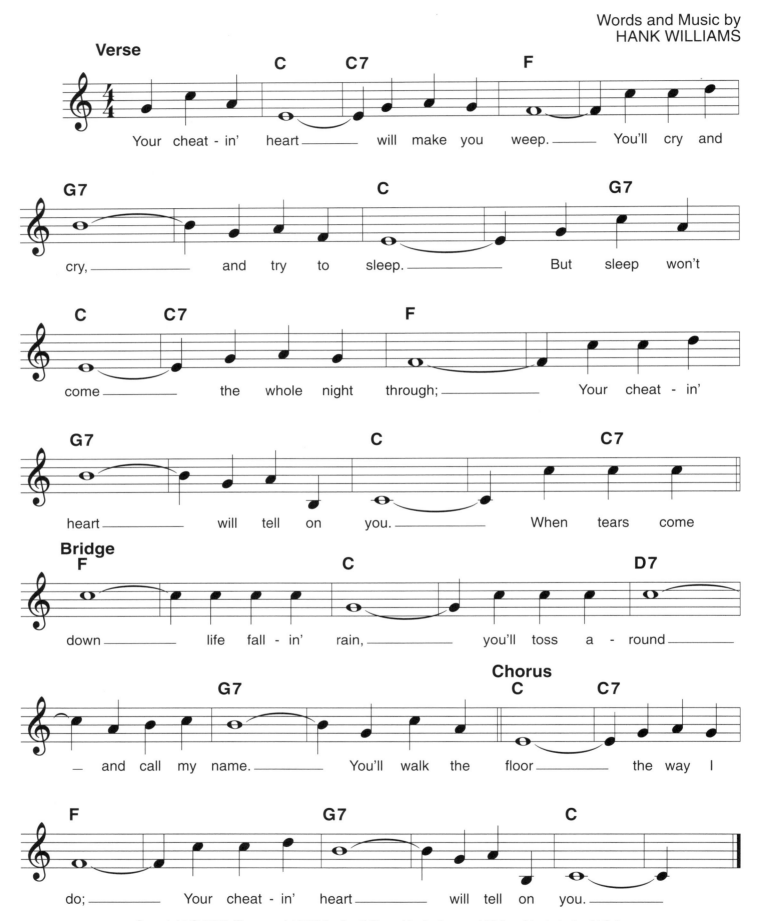

All My Loving

Words and Music by
JOHN LENNON and PAUL McCARTNEY

Love Me Tender

Words and Music by
ELVIS PRESLEY and VERA MATSON

Verse

1. Love me ten - der, love me sweet; nev - er let me go. You have made my life com - plete, and I love you so.
2. Love me ten - der, love me long; take me to your heart. For it's there that I be - long, and we'll nev - er part.
3. Love me ten - der, love me dear; tell me you are mine. I'll be yours through all the years, till the end of time.

Chorus

Love me ten - der, love me true, all my dreams ful - fill. For my dar - lin' I love you,

1., 2. and I al - ways will.

3. and I al - ways will.

Bye Bye Love

Words and Music by FELICE BRYANT
and BOUDLEAUX BRYANT

NOWHERE MAN

Words and Music by
JOHN LENNON and PAUL McCARTNEY

Chorus

He's a real no - where man, sit - ting in his

no - where land, mak - ing all his no - where plans for

To Coda ⊕ **Verse**

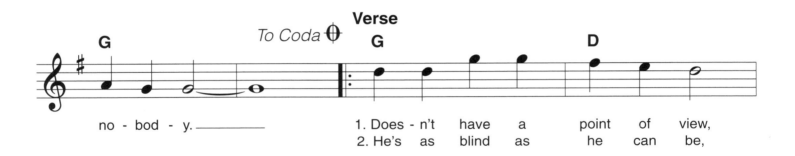

no - bod - y. _____

1. Does - n't have a point of view,
2. He's as blind as he can be,

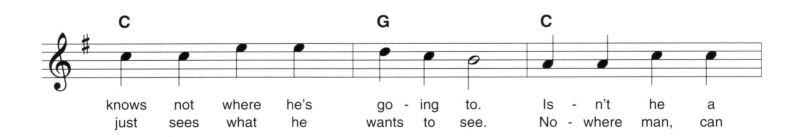

knows not where he's go - ing to. Is - n't he a
just sees what he wants to see. No - where man, can

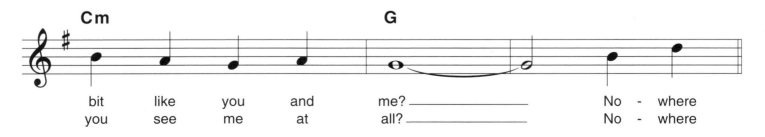

bit like you and me? _____ No - where
you see me at all? _____ No - where

Bridge

Bm   C   Bm

man, please lis - ten. You don't know what you're
man, please don't wor - ry. Take your time, _____ don't

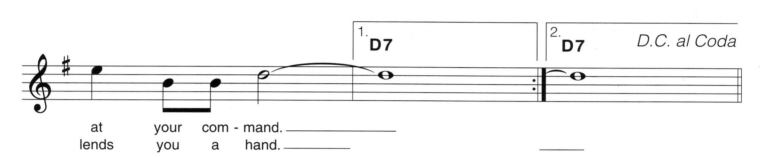

C   Bm   G   *eighth note*

miss - ing. No - where man, the world _____ is
hur - ry. Leave it all till some - bod - y else _____

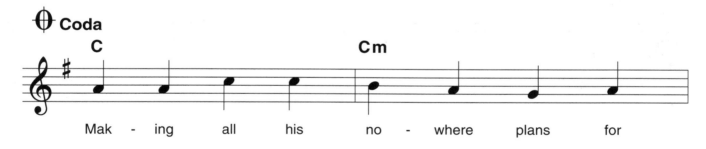

1. D7   2. D7   *D.C. al Coda*

at your com - mand. _____
lends you a hand. _____

Coda

C   Cm

Mak - ing all his no - where plans for

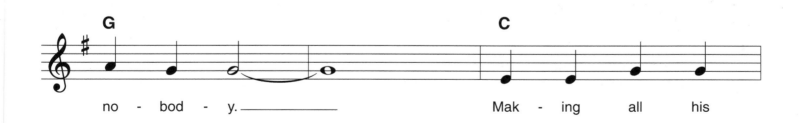

G   C

no - bod - y. _____ Mak - ing all his

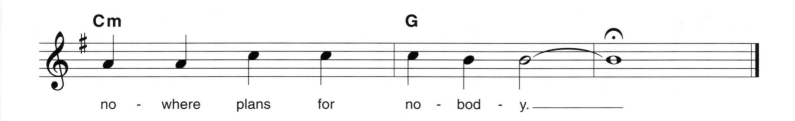

Cm   G

no - where plans for no - bod - y. _____

Stand By Me

Words and Music by
BEN E. KING, JERRY LEIBER and MIKE STOLLER

EVERY BREATH YOU TAKE

Written and Composed by
STING

THE SOUND OF SILENCE

Words and Music by
PAUL SIMON

Additional Lyrics

2. In restless dreams I walked alone
Narrow streets of cobblestone,
'Neath the halo of a street lamp,
I turned my collar to the cold and damp
When my eyes were stabbed
By the flash of a neon light
That split the night
And touched the sound of silence.

3. And in the naked light I saw
Ten thousand people, maybe more.
People talking without speaking,
People hearing without listening,
People writing songs that voices never share
And no one dare
Disturb the sound of silence.

BORN TO BE WILD

Words and Music by
MARS BONFIRE

I SHOT THE SHERIFF

Words and Music by
BOB MARLEY

Low Rider

Words and Music by SYLVESTER ALLEN, HAROLD R. BROWN,
MORRIS DICKERSON, JERRY GOLDSMITH, LEROY JORDAN,
LEE OSKAR, CHARLES W. MILLER and HOWARD SCOTT

IMAGINE

Words and Music by
JOHN LENNON

die for   and no re - li - gion too. ___
hun - ger,   a broth - er - hood of man. ___

Im - ag - ine all   the   peo - ple   liv - ing life in
Im - ag - ine all   the   peo - ple   shar - ing all the

Chorus

peace. }   You, _____   you may say I'm a
world. }

dream - er,   but I'm not the on - ly one.

I hope some day ___ you'll join ___ us

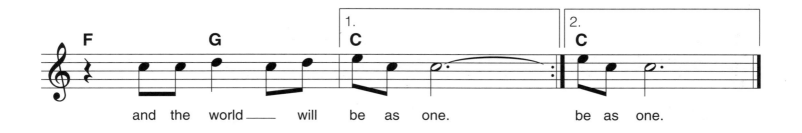

and the world ___ will be as one.   be as one.

Your Song

Words and Music by
ELTON JOHN and BERNIE TAUPIN

New note:
B♭

BROWN EYED GIRL

Words and Music by
VAN MORRISON

Additional Lyrics

2. Whatever happened to Tuesday and so slow,
   Going down the old mine with a transistor radio?
   Standing in the sunlight laughing,
   Hiding behind a rainbow's wall,
   Slipping and a-sliding
   All along the waterfall
   With you, my brown eyed girl.
   You, my brown eyed girl.
   Do you remember when we used to sing;

3. So hard to find my way, now that I'm all on my own.
   I saw you just the other day, my, how you have grown.
   Cast my memory back there, Lord,
   Sometimes I'm overcome thinking 'bout it.
   Making love in the green grass
   Behind the stadium
   With you, my brown eyed girl.
   You, my brown eyed girl.
   Do you remember when we used to sing;

MR. TAMBOURINE MAN

Words and Music by
BOB DYLAN

Verse

1. Take me for — a trip up - on — your — ma-gic swirl - ling —
(2.) read - y to — go an - y - where. — I'm — read - y for — to —

ship, all my sen - ses have been — stripped, and my hands —
fade un - to — my own par - ade, cast your danc -

— can't feel to — grip, and my toes — too numb to —
- ing spell my —

step, wait-ing on - ly for my boot heels to — be wan -

- der - ing. 2. I'm way. I

D.S. al Coda

pro - mise to — go un - der it.

Coda
Outro
N.C. (D)

Repeat and fade

you.

BREAK ON THROUGH TO THE OTHER SIDE

Words and Music by
THE DOORS

1. You know the day de - stroys the night, ___
2. We chased our pleas - ures here, ___
3. I found an is - land in your arms, ___

night di - vides ___ the day. ___ Tried to run, ___
dug our treas - ures there. ___ Can you still re - call ___ the
coun - try in ___ your eyes. ___ Arms that chain, ___

tried to hide. ___ }
time we cried? ___ } Break on through ___ to the oth - er side. ___
eyes that lie. ___ }

To Coda ⊕

Break on through ___ to the oth - er side. ___ Break on through ___ to the

1.

2.

oth - er side. ___

WALK DON'T RUN

By JOHNNY SMITH